D0907853

honeycomb heart

PRAYERS, POEMS & OFFERINGS FOR THE JOURNEY

Written by Kael Klassen

Grayhorse Publishing, 2019
Fernie, BC

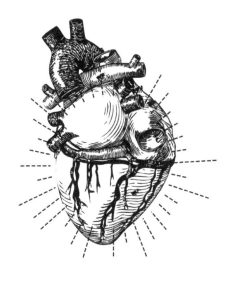

i dedicate this book to myself.
to the courage, the honesty and the diligence it has taken,
continues to take,
in order to heal.
i dedicate this book to those of you that are doing the same.

bibliomancy

i was going to give each of the offerings contained within these pages their own title.
i was also going to try to break them into categories.
maybe by prayer, poem or offering.
maybe by mood and tone.
maybe by darkness and light.
but it never felt right to do any of that.
because, like my own honeycomb heart, it feels very difficult to categorize or compartmentalize or narrow down what is held within these pages.
because, like my own honeycomb heart, it feels best just to offer a container and then let the nourishment and bustle overflow from there.
so, sweet beast, i hope that you read this book page by page, cover to cover.
i do.
but even more so, i hope you simply hold in your own heart that what you need is what you will receive as you flip through at random.
i hope that this book is a source of healing; a soothing balm for your own honeycomb heart.
i hope that this book lets you know you are not alone; that it provides the relief of companionship.
thank you. for doing your big work and, in doing so, equipping yourself with the tools you need in any given moment to keep going on your own spiral path toward your truth.
xo
kael

i am kael.
daughter of beth.
granddaughter of hilda and katie.
great granddaughter of katharina and anna, catherine and
aganetha.
i am a mighty warrior.
daughter of one consecrated to god.
granddaughter of a woman of battle and a woman of purity.
great granddaughter of purity, grace and holiness.
i am a mighty warrior.
on my horse of midnight sky. snake coiled, body taut,
around my left wrist. barn owl perched, talons gripping, on
my right hand. and a mahogany crone, ancient and rich as
mountain topography, enrobed in garnets and indigo, at my
side.
i am a mighty warrior.
i have found my way to consecration with the goddess.
i am a woman of battle.
i am holy in this feminine form.
i am fumbling my way with grace.
sometimes our two bodies move rhythmically,
synchronized to something resonant my ears cannot hear.
sometimes grace dances on, all laughter and light, ease and
ability, humbleness and humility; her feet delighting in the
mud, her hands deftly crowning the chaos with flowers,
while the bones of this life crunch sweetly between her
sharp teeth as she sucks back the marrow of it all.
she dances on while i watch and stumble after her; tripping
and falling, finding myself mired in the muck of one human
mess or another.
but i see grace.

i found my way to see her, to recognize her for the beast she truly is rather than the immaculately groomed and thoroughly untouchable virtue i always thought her to be.
and now purity.
the ancestral line of my grandmothers contains a lot of purity.
i can feel myself recoil from purity.
but i am a mighty warrior.
i have a horse and a snake, a barn owl and a crone, and we will find my way to the truth in purity.
still, i don't want to.
i roll the word around in my mouth and want to spit it out.
i can feel it slide, thick and heavy, past my clenched teeth, down my closing throat and land heavy in my belly; a long forgotten ember of shame waking from dormancy.
but i am a mighty warrior and i will honour each spine that forms this ancestral line.
i will hone and heal, polish and mend.
until vertebra by vertebra this great spine of my women extends straight and strong, holy and potent, from root to crown.
and so it is.

one

i am not here to play small.
i am not here to dim the light of the universe shining in me.
i am not here to pretend i am anything less than the ecstatic
dance of the divine in conscious form.
i am not here to hush my voice or soften the unabashed
laughter that tumbles, straight from my belly, out my
mouth.
i am not here to colour inside the lines of how a nice girl
ought to behave.
i am not here to satisfy any expectations but those of my
wild, sacred spirit.
i am not here to languish in indifference or wallow in apathy.
no.
i am here to make a difference.
i am here to brush my fingers ever so lightly, tenderly, along
the walls of any box i have been put in, before knocking
them to the ground; stepping from the dust and the debris
of that prison with my heart blazing.
i am here to rise from the ashes of who i was over and over;
each time burning more brightly, with more strength, with
more wisdom and with more truth.
i am here to push every edge, cross every boundary and
erase every line drawn in the proverbial sand.
i am here to lead the way, to hold the space and to clear the
wreckage.
i am here to hold the flame of a holy and purposeful anger in
the face of the violence and abuse we have endured.
i am here to unearth what was stolen from us.
and i am here to do it all, again and again, for as long as it
takes.
and so it is.

two

memento mori
{latin: remember that you must die}

because sometimes we need the reminder to allow for all of
the little deaths.
the death of limiting belief systems.
the death of low vibrational relationships.
the death of "should".
the death of isolation and fear.
the death of imitation.
the death of lack.
the death of comparison.
the death of thinking before feeling.
the death of who we think we are supposed to be, or who we
pretend to be, in order to make room for the rebirth of who
we truly are.
all of these deaths, sometimes sweet and sometimes
excruciating, are our ways in; the ways that we can
surrender ourselves to the unlearning, unbecoming, and
unravelling of all that does not ring with the clarity of our
heart's truth.
the ways that we can shed the skin of all that feels too tight
or rubs and chafes at our soft and beautiful true self.
we all have to die, sometimes a thousand times in just one
day.
but we also all get to be reborn again and again and again.
until one day we finally arrive full circle at who, under all of
the clutter we picked up along the way, we have always been.

three

gather your treasures,
your talismans,
your sacred reminders.
then sit, sweet child.
rest in the totality of your self.
with each breath in, nourish.
with each breath out, release.
become so quiet,
so still,
that you can feel each heartbeat singing you home.
there is nowhere you need to be.
there is nothing you need to do.
you are safe.
you are held.
you are creation.
and you are waking up.
i am.
you are.
and so it is.

four

i'll wait here.
my soles could grow roots; nosing and nudging their way
through the clay, clinging, not desperately, but
determinedly, to the bedrock of this land.
and i would be held.
anchored.
a sentinel amongst the sentinels.
or maybe i could lay down, lay still, and let the spongey
expanse of my lungs become moss.
my heart would become the most exquisitely formed heart-
shaped rock; a treasure hidden in the forest.
my hair, lichen.
my skin, just another expanse of forest floor; unremarkable
and yet entirely holy.
my bones could offer a framework for all that needs a safe
place to land, a safe place to begin.
or maybe something less permanent.
like a night on a bed of moss under a blanket of stars.
or a hushed moment, no longer than the cycle of a breath in
and then out again.
or just a blink of the eye; but a slow blink, because the way
the clouds have become tangled in my eyelashes makes my
lids heavy.
i would wait there.

five

we are so brilliant at holding space for the "good".
we feel joy, love, gratitude, kindness, excitement, hope,
bliss, and so on.
we feel all of these society-approved, positive feelings so
fully and then, just as easily as we receive them, we release
them.
we don't shamefully bury joy.
we don't agonize over gratitude.
we don't get stuck in a downward spiral of bliss.
we don't feel embarrassed by hope.
but fear? guilt? anger? shame? grief? jealousy? despair?
frustration? doubt?
there is a whole host of these emotional experiences that
our world has deemed less than.
emotions that we feel obligated to hide, to wade through on
our own, and to never let see the light of day.
emotions that, by association, we assume make us less than.
there is no quick fix to this.
instead there is steady awareness.
gentle, tender, steady awareness.
of self.
of the choices we make. and that, always, we contain the gift
of choice.
of our ability to soften into the entirety of our experience.
to allow for the entirety of our experience.
of our ability to gather in community and be heard, felt and
seen.
of the fact that life is happening for us, not to us.
of our selves as something so much bigger and more
beautiful than just this human vessel.

so for all of you, everywhere, i offer this blessing:

you are safe.

you are held.

you are love.

you are the wisdom of your pure and sacred heart.

you are the vast infinity of your soul.

you are the ecstatic dance of the divine, exploring herself in physical form.

you are the roots in the mud and the blossom striving for the sun.

you are the perfect expression of a benevolent and loving universe.

you are the vessel of creation.

and you?

you are holy ground.

and so it is.

six

i move through the room.
the amorphous auras of energy cling to me.
or slink away from me.
all these gaping wounds hidden behind platitudes and
shining eyes, masks and half truths.
all these gaping wounds walking a fine line.
on the one side, believing that they're contained. believing
their own lies. believing that no one can see them. that if
they just keep talking about the weather and moving
through the motions of expected human form they will fake
it till they make it and won't it be fun to have cake at the end
of this elaborate masquerade ball we call a life.
and on the other side, the yearning to shriek and to howl. to
scream the guttural syllables that are churning up from
deep within bellies and hearts. to itch and tear at skin that
has become tighter and tighter and thinner and thinner as it
tries to contain the lies piling up on top of the truths. the
desperation to be seen and heard and touched. the
remembrance of stardust and soul breathing life to skin and
bone. the longing to be reclaimed by the ancestors they can
hear whispering to them when they wake in witching hour.
a fine line.
on one side, the labour of containment and denial.
on the other, the ache and agony of waking up; of
remembrance.
but now the music is loud and the bass is strong and we all
fall into a rhythmic seething mass.
no fine lines.
no balancing act of concealing truth or lies.
just bodies dancing each other higher and higher.

seven

i am slower.
sweeter.
softer.
an unfurling of wild edges.
an exploration of liminal spaces.
reassembled flesh and bone, sinew and skin; new but not
new, same but different.
humming honeycomb heart.
deep taproot anchored to the earth's core.
but also furtive tendrils seeking purchase, nourishment,
and new ground.
rich, prolific mossy forest floor.
dark endless starry night sky expansion.
selkie whispers, shedding human form for animal
remembrance.
intuitive body.
wisdom body.
wide awake, holy body.
cellular remembrance.
listening. heeding. course correcting.
i am softer, sweeter, slower.
an unfurling of wild edges.
i am.
you are.
and so it is.

you, dear beautiful creature, i want to tell you stories; my
stories.
these stories keep welling up within me. but, just as i reach
for them, they slip through my fingers, as insubstantial as
smoke.
one story starts with how i found a baby jackrabbit in the
window well. a jackrabbit so small she fit in the palm of my
hand with room to spare. how her tiny heart, a heart no
bigger than a honeybee, thudded against my palm. how i set
her free in the park, because that's what the internet said
you did with a wild baby rabbit, but how i sobbed and in the
darkness of night i went back out, like a wild wailing thing,
and scoured the grass looking for her.
and there is the story of when the trees told me to seek the
crone. and i found her; deep in the darkest part of the forest.
how she bound me to her, in service of her, with the rune ior
scratched over the temple of my heart. how her hands are
rich mahogany and wrinkled like the topography of
mountain tops and river valleys. how she and i are snake
and barn owl and ancient matrilineal line. how i feel she is
lilith, but she owes me no answers and so i cannot be sure.
i want to tell you the story of sedna's voice; how she sounds
like deep water moving over even deeper rocks; like
something ancient. and then lament that i don't hear her
anymore.
or stories about holding the sweet heaviness of my children
as they twitch and sigh their way into sleep.
there are stories upon stories teeming and seething in me;
lately i feel more story than person.
but none of the stories are complete.
or maybe they are. but not in the neat and tidy sense of a
beginning, a middle, and an ending.

these are bread crumb stories. each one leading me further down the path, deeper into the forest, and higher up the mountain.

these are lifetime stories.

and maybe, i think, i want to share my stories so that i don't feel so alone.

so that you will hear me and see me and help put human flesh to my bones, anchoring me here and now.

so that i don't float off, a swarm of words that won't add up until i reach the end.

so that in this moment there is sense and meaning.

or at least companionship.

you, dear beautiful creature, i want to tell you stories.

nine

i loved you.
and then i didn't.
i don't think it happened all at once.
but one day i noticed that my teeth hurt from chewing on
the brittle emptiness of your words.
and then i noticed that my belly, once soft and lovely, had
become hollow and hard. because, for all the promises you
brandished, you refused to nourish me.
and then my heart.
my heart, once a hive of honeybee activity in your hands,
grew silent at the mere thought of you; void of that thrum
and swarm and sweetness you used to invoke.
my body, this wild animal of instinctual knowing, she knew.
in so many ways my body knew.
and once a body knows, it's only a matter of time before
mind catches up. or can no longer turn a blind eye.
and just like that you were gone from me.
all at once in that way that actually happens slowly, quietly,
over time.
and sometimes my cells sigh at the memory of you.
and that's ok. because memories are the stories that
mattered, that still hold gifts.
and sometimes my being still sings, sometimes sweetly,
sometimes with fire, calling out to the places that you used
to live.
but you don't live here anymore.
now you are just one more who couldn't meet my strength;
my courage and honesty.
one more who played at knight in shining armour.
but we both knew i was your joan of arc and you were
simply drawn like a moth to my fire.
one more who i could not dim myself for.

so here i am again.

this familiar place.

burning versions and pieces of me, falsehoods, to the ground.

releasing realities that will never, could never, exist.

rolling the taste of disappointment over my tongue; familiar but not bitter.

because this time i see the lessons for what they are.

no confusion.

no head in the sand.

no denial.

i see clearly the teaching of us and i honour it.

still, here i am again.

peeling off layers and masks.

knocking down more walls.

destroying the corner you backed me into.

because this is me.

and i have work to do with this lifetime.

this is me.

no longer dancing to the melody of your fear and resistance.

this is me.

holy and potent and rising.

this is me.

and i thank you. i do.

but you don't live here anymore.

ten

do not offer me your love and light unless you are willing to
also offer me your grief and rage.
because love and light without grief and rage are just
platitudes.
without grief and rage there is no marrow.
no meat.
no gristle.
nothing for me to sharpen the teeth of my heart against.
give me love and light, certainly.
but let it be nourished,
let it be fuelled,
and let it be made real
by your grief and rage.

eleven

listen.
if you never find your way to physical, mental or emotional
stillness, how will you attune to your spirit's movement?
find stillness.
physically. mentally. emotionally.
and then you will find your spirit's movement.
the way her serpent body can coil, languid or ready to strike.
the way her wings can float on the air currents of entire
solar systems, beat rapid fire and iridescent like a
hummingbird, or flick flutter transparent like a honeybee.
the way she can move sure and steady or fast and
thunderous, like wild hoof beats, through any terrain.
the way her fascia expands and contracts in perfect
harmony to the flex and dance of her muscles; skin
stretching and sinew lengthening.
the twitch of her hide as she shrugs off the minutiae.
all of it.
all of her movements a story.
no; all of her movements a map.
she travels with grace and grit, skipping and dancing,
trudging and labouring, along a path your human mind
denies by foolishly pretending to be bereft and alone.
quiet everything else.
relax the hum of your physical body.
tune out the din of your mental body.
soften the ache and anguish of your emotional body.
and then attune,
wholly,
holy,
to the movement, the map, of your spiritual body.

twelve

everything is an elder, she wrote me.

and i believe her, i do.

i can even see the way her crystal blue eyes would flutter as she says it, her voice dropping lower, slower, potent with a truth that is not of this plane.

everything is an elder.

everything is a teacher.

and i know.

i know how even when i sit in the role of teacher or healer i am just as fully in the space of student.

i know how every rock and every tree, every mossy forest floor and every mountain top, those twinkling stars and fiery sunrises, and every everything in between are my elders.

still, some days, how potent the loss of a home is for me.

that latent sting of being an orphan of no culture.

so i collect the pieces as i go.

gathering the threads that create my story; weaving my own braid of who i am and where i came from, lifetime to lifetime. hope welling in my heart that i am doing it right.

and i guess that is the crux of it right there; i am not mourning the loss of a teacher or an elder, my life is rich with both; within and without.

no, i am mourning the loss of a wayfinder. the loss of a hand-holder. the loss of some benevolent, wise grandmother who has journeyed this exact path and can show me the way.

but how could such a person exist?

me, this existence, this experience, these strands of dna and these cellular memories are mine and mine alone.

there is no one who can give me a map to navigate this course.

no one to give me explicit directions from point a to point z.
but there are scores of teachers and elders. an entire web of
lightworkers, guides and guardians. a world full of sacred
space holders and holy soul members.
so do i mourn for what simply cannot exist?
or do i rejoice with gratitude for what i am immersed in?
i choose gratitude.
and in that choice i shift again, always, to faith.
faith that these threads i collect and weave are honouring
the story that sang for a voice; my voice.
faith that i never journey alone.
faith that i can shapeshift, expand and land into the skin
and bones of my soul.
faith that no matter where i go, home is where i am.
and so it is.

thirteen

grief is good, she tells me.
grief is a holy fire lighting the way.
grief is your tumultuous magpie heart letting you know
what mattered.
what matters still.
she tells me so many things these days.
and i am listening, i am.
but i am also so tired.
and when i look around, with my wide eyes and tear-stained
cheeks, and i am shrouded in smoke, ankle deep in ash and
running my fingertips over the rubble of these crumbling
facades, i cannot help but feel small.
and an unfathomable exhaustion.
because the rebuild has barely begun.
because this, so far, has simply been the release.
but she's still here.
her voice soothing and steady, ancient; like stones being
tumbled by water.
she's still here.
lifting my chin so that my eyes catch the light.
holding me to her and working, no, weaving her stories
through me.
she's still here.
in my reverence to the forest floor.
and the thunderstorms in my hips.
and my reclamation song.
and my well of creation.
and every drum beat.
and the length of my spine.
and each cellular memory.
and every awakening.

and the prayers that fall, sometimes soft like petals and
sometimes electric like lightning, from my lips, my hands
and my heart.
she's still here.
she was always here.
and here she shall remain.

fourteen

she calls me to the forest and so, of course, i go.
but not my usual forest.
no sun dappled velvet floor. no cooling respite. no lush beds
of moss or fern. no heady scent of cedar. no crystal clear
creek winding happily and noisily about.
today she calls me to the forest of the vultures.
where the expanse of blue sky overhead is endless and
unmerciful; too bright, too big, too blue.
where trees are sparse and the grass is baked golden under
the unyielding eye of the sun.
where the big ponderosa grow; their scent baked thick and
sweet into the air.
where the vultures are.
it's not my usual forest, but i know it well and love it dear.
so i go.
i lay my flesh down against the earth.
i feel the brittle snap and poke of dry grass against my skin
as i settle in, settle down, and listen.
listen to tinny clicks and chirps of the grasshoppers.
listen to the brittle rattle of seed pods as they dance lazily in
the rising currents of hot air.
listen to scrabble of tiny mouse feet over fallen logs and the
hum of dragonfly wings overhead.
listen to the sudden absence of sound.
listen, alert now, to the swish and whistle of big wings
slicing through thick air.
i don't open my eyes, but i hear them land; the flapping of
wings in descent and then the thud of large taloned feet
meeting parched earth.
one. two. three.
they're all here.

i know why she sent me here.
the vultures have been showing up, waiting, on the edges of
my vision for months now.
their piecing amber gold eyes and scarlet heads such a
contrast against the deep oil spill hues of their feathered
cloaks.
i know why she sent me here.
i let them come.
not afraid or alarmed; they feel familiar by now.
i let them come.
and they set to work immediately.
picking the decay and the rot from my being.
consuming the spaces that have been allowed to fester.
they work quietly.
efficiently.
the absolute silence of that seared forest punctuated only
by the occasional click of a craggy beak or rustle of inky
feathers.
and just like that, in what may have been no more than five
minutes or an eternity or both, they are done.
they've left what is healthy.
in places, many places, they've gorged themselves all the
way down to the bone; leaving my skeleton frame clean and
shimmering, polished and pearlescent, ready to anchor
whatever new growth seeks purchase.
and as the three take flight, the disc of the moon slips in
front of the sun; two star crossed lovers meet.
and that oven of a forest cools noticeably.
and the garish bright of the day dims intensely.
and the air that moments before felt so thick, becomes light
and soft as silk.
and finally she is here with me.

in this anomaly of time, this moment of midday cool and
dark, she arrives.
she places a tiny blue robin's egg in my throat.
she offers a prayer that i can't quite hear.
but i feel my crown open and expand, the fibres of my form
sing with currents new and unknown, and i find myself
whispering:
i know my ways of creation.
i am the womb of god.
and so it is.

gather the women. bring back the goddess.
she told me.
tells me.
what is my work in this lifetime?
i had asked.
gather the women. bring back the goddess.
she replied.
and i did.
but then i burnt out.
but then i became intimidated.
but then i fixated on feigned fragility.
gather the women. bring back the goddess.
yes.
i feel this,
this directive,
this decree,
unfurling in new ways now.
augmenting dna.
activating star codes.
sharpening the canines of my heart.
pulsing through blood and bone and breath.
it won't look like what your mind expects.
she chastises. reminds.
all the same:
gather the women. bring back the goddess.
she insists.
gather the women. bring back the goddess.
i am.
i will.
and so it is.

dissident daughter, she says.

i've been watching you.

i watched the way you danced your way out onto the thin ice;
all youthful folly and unenlightened bravado, your eyes
twinkling and your chin defiant.

i watched when you fell through.

the way it matured you almost instantly.

the way, as your feet sank into the strata of untouched
detritus at that frozen lake floor, your hair became
weightless, dancing with the micro currents, wreathing
your surprised face; a crown befitting a deep water medusa.

no, a deep water sedna.

oh sweet child, my crone in the making, i watched you
waver.

that split second eternity of uncertainty: would you stay
down there and marry your self to the murky depths or
would you kick your way back up to once again breathe air
into your lungs.

and just like that your strong legs thrashed.

your arms beat ferociously against viscous icy water as you
winged your way upward.

i watched you breach the surface of that frozen space, that
threshold space.

the way you gulped air deep into your watery lungs while
looking, wide-eyed and blinking, at both the newness and
familiarity of the world around you; a space you had
occupied so surely moments before, yet also a space you
couldn't quite recall ever knowing.

i watched as who you were in those silty watery depths
became enmeshed with who you still believed yourself to be,
as she, in turn, became enmeshed with who you now had
become.

i watched as you shapeshifted to embody all of these versions and visions of you.
the way that overwhelmed you.
the way you keened and wailed.
how the effort of becoming and unbecoming caused you to shudder and writhe.
the way the howls rose, raw and rasping, from your belly, through your heart, past the gatekeeper of your golden throat, prying loose your clenched teeth to escape beyond your lips.
i watched.
i watched you crawl back to solid ground.
i watched you gather your selves as you stood to walk two-legged on an earth that was as familiar as it was alien to you.
i watched.
i watch.
i am always here.
dissident daughter, my darling brat, i have always been here.

seventeen

i touched down gently, intentionally.
roots, offerings, to the mycelium.
whispering soft prayers to not meet a bear as i walked with
these four hundred year old beings.
feet on ground.
breath in body.
prayers find fertile ground.

eighteen

today, swimming in the cold of a spring fed lake, rain drops
falling all around me, i mapped the country of my body.
the ache of love lost, missed, and yearned for, lives tucked
under the tips of my shoulder blades; waiting like wings
that might unfurl at any moment.
the bowl of my pelvis, full of creation; stories longing to be
told, stories longing to be healed.
my holy "no" like a shining gem at the base of my throat and
my radiant "yes" rippling like wildfire through my chest.
the length of my spine, from the tip of my tailbone to the
base of my skull, spirit and divine energy dance. a dance so
familiar and so foreign at the same time; something half
remembered here in this lifetime.
in my hips i hold the storm clouds of hurt.
roots grow down, strong and sacred like redwoods, from the
base of my pelvis and out the soles of my feet.
the curve of my belly, my softest, strongest energetic
processing centre.
pangs of emotions so strong that they catch my breath,
pulse through the rhythm of my lungs.
and at the centre is my heart; my well of knowing, my truest
and most trusted guidance.
the temple of my body.
my geography.
the landscape of my spirit.

nineteen

i am not your rib.
no.
i denounce such foolishness.
i refuse to believe that i, a magnificence of flux and flow,
have roots in an origin story that tells me i am an
afterthought.
i refuse to believe that the magnitudes held within the
elasticity of my being were created from rigid bone alone.
i refuse the notion that i come from the cage of a man, when
man so willingly let my line shoulder the burden of being
cast from the garden; left us to wear the prison garb of
temptress, sinner, witch, subservient and whore.
i refuse.
because i?
i am the softness, the richness, and the expansiveness of the
womb.
i am cycles of both potent fertility and exquisite shedding
aligned with the moon herself.
i am the perpetual rhythm and pulse of oceans past, present
and future.
i am the cleaving of tectonic plates as the earth labours to
give birth to herself.
i am the ecstasy of supernovas.
i am.
all of that is contained within this vessel.
do not reduce my origin story to the brittle hardness of one
rib, taken from the cage of one man.

twenty

at the intersection of faith, folly, hope and despair:
me,
looking forward to the next lifetime
so that i can love you again.

twenty-one

i have sung your name to my heart.
i have whispered it to the creatures with wings.
i have called your name in my dreamspace and delighted
that there, at least there, you respond.
i have dropped your name like breadcrumbs,
pulled it around me like armour,
and ridden it into battle like some great warhorse;
hoping fervently that it would lead me through the forest,
keep me safe, and carry me through the battlefield.
carry me home.
but the wild woman goddess within me throws her head
back and shrieks with laughter, grief, and rage.
because, silly child, only my own name can do all of that.
i have howled your syllables at the moon; sad and lonely, a
keening cry that leaves me bereft for days.
i have torn your title from my flesh, cursing the suffocating
way it cloaks me, shadows me, and engulfs me.
i have pulled the thorn of your name from my body the
same way a wild animal would; chewing and worrying at the
wound left behind.
i have spat your name from my mouth and quickly inhaled
other words; trying to fill every space so that you cannot
sneak back in; trying to learn to love the shape and taste of
some other word.
i have carried you.
in joy and in remembrance,
in rage and in confusion,
in frustration,
i have carried you.
but only once, tonight, i wrote your name.
i wrote each letter of your name, carefully, mindfully,
lovingly, on a silvery sage leaf.

and then i set you on fire and watched the smoke carry you
away from me.
and now i sit with sadness. but she is an old friend of mine
and i don't mind her company.
and now i can feel a faint fire burning; my own, clean and
bright, straight from my roots.
and now i sing my own name into my heart.

twenty-two

we needed to wash our bones.
somehow cobwebs and dust had amassed in our hollows.
somehow our collective and individual joints had become
harsh and abrasive; rubbing to the point of, at best,
aggravation and, at worst, a deep and gnawing ache.
somehow rust was forming and corrosion was happening
and we were slipping through the holes in each other's
frames.
somehow life happened and we got dirty, played dirty, and
we needed a good soak.
to you, my love, for getting dirty but recognizing the being
of dirt from the playing of dirt; the integrity versus the
dishonesty and the wallowing in delight versus the
floundering in abjectivity.
to you.
my love.

twenty-three

i'm glad you got back up.
but now tell me, what have you learned?
don't feed me platitudes.
offer me the gristle, the meat and the marrow of what you
have learned.
what is congruent?
what is cohesive?
what have you sharpened the teeth of your heart against?
what has satiated the hollowness that filled the creative
centre of your belly?
what sticks like a thorn in your mind?
what leaves you thirsting for more?
what, tell me, have you learned?

twenty-four

i thought i lost my way.
i didn't.
i found myself a new way without even realizing it and it
just took some time to get reoriented.
i bet you did too.
but now i am reoriented.
now i recalibrate.
now i recentre. regroup. reground.
now i realign with my path.
and for the first time in an excruciatingly long time, i feel
hope lift up and away from her perch in my rib cage.
the feathery flick of her wings against my heart.
the rise of her warbling song in my throat.
the lightness and ease, the grace, of her crescendoing dance
along the air currents in my lungs.
ripples of ecstatic joy spread as the rest of my body
responds to her brilliant plumage.
hope has taken flight.

twenty-five

i am remembering my ways of creation.
listening in.
summoning the spine.
barn owl clutching my right hand.
snake intertwining my left.
a black horse made of midnight sky beneath me.
my throat is stretching, expanding, evolving.
and i am remembering where i came from.
i see the length of my ancestral line.
i see my points of origin.
i am remembering all the way back.
all the way back now.
to when i created at the cellular level; star codes and
guidance tattooed like a map over my skin.
to when i roamed wild and powerful and holy in my female
form on the land.
to the times i have studied at the feet of the crone and to the
times when the crone was me.
i close my eyes and my body instantly shifts.
energy shifts.
spirit shifts.
spine and snake and barn owl riding the midnight sky.
crone and creatress.
wild and holy and potent.
stardust and star codes and skin.
all of it.
dancing together and apart.
mingling through memory and dna and dreamscape.
i am reclaiming my ways of creation.

twenty-six

i stood in front of the home you've built; with your white
picket fence and the perfect curtains framing pristine
windows.
but this time i looked closer.
this time i could see the places where paint had been
slathered on thick; a quick fix to shroud the decay.
the places where neat and tidy beds of roses sat pretty in
front of a crumbling foundation.
i stood.
wind whipping my hair in front of my eyes.
grass twining around my ankles.
my heart keening in my throat.
and i studied.
i studied you.
i studied your foundation.
i had one match left and i wanted to use that match on you.
to burn your foundation to true ground.
to expose you.
to free you, maybe.
to hurt you, definitely.
i could see, i could feel and i could hear the way the flames
would lick their way up the walls you've built; languorous
and fluid as they consumed your facade.
but i turned on my heel.
i turned my back on your white picket fence and your
beautiful curtains.
i turned away and i struck my match on a stone.
i held her small flicker to the sky; in reverence, in gratitude,
and in prayer.
and then i dropped that match to the ground.
i felt my last match land at my feet.

i felt her flames, languorous and fluid, begin to climb me.
and i felt her feast on all of the places that you still exist in
me; the tender places that still hold love, the raw places
anchored in hurt, the hard places tamping down denial and
the places aching, screaming, and writhing with anger.
even though hell hath no fury, i did not burn you down.
i burned you away.
and now i step not from my own ashes, but from the ashes
of where i wore you, of where i carried you.
and now, old friend, good-bye.
because this is the last time that i burn for you.

sticks and stones anchor my bones and names can only fuel
me.
and the bridges i burn light my way as i mend the crack
where you broke my mother's back.
and her mother's.
and her mother's mother's.
the bridges i burn light my way as i mend the crack where
you broke our ancestral spine.
the bridges i burn light my way as i weave copper and gold
through vertebrae that are as old as time.
as i fill fractures with tourmaline, mica and moonstone.
as i patch the spaces rubbed raw and the places worn down
with the lush fecundity of mossy beds.
as i sing over the bones of my lineage.
as i sing down the bones of my line.
i mend the crack where you broke our back.
i spin and weave and cast a web over that chasm; carrying
my sisters, i weave us back to who we were before.
before you broke so many backs.
before you robbed and smothered and denied the holy
feminine fire that was never about you.
never for you.
but still it scared you.
because, like any coward, you were too blind to see that our
fire had room to warm you too.
like any coward, you robbed and smothered and denied us.
because you couldn't bare to see such strength and beauty,
such magnificence, while your own spine, gnarled and
twisted where rich nourishment once flowed, rattled hollow
against your rib cage.
so you created the crack and broke our back.

but now, sticks and stones anchor my bones.
but now, names fuel me.
and now?
these bridges i burn light my way.

twenty-eight

what do you want? she asks.
again, so often lately, the words are right there, tumbling
from my heart through my throat and out my mouth like a
raucous parliament of magpies; vibrant, loud, slightly
abrasive and entirely impossible to ignore.
i want purpose and passion and peace.
i want to not feel trapped.
i want humankind to wake up, to do better.
i want my blue-eyed boy to weep a little less and my hazel-
eyed boy to defy a little less.
i want to feel at home.
i want to be content here and now.
i want to stop seeking something that i may not be able to
find on this earthly plane, in this flesh and blood.
i want healing; theirs and mine.
i want to be released; from trauma and grief, from belief
systems and patterning, from ancestral wounds.
i want to be released. free.
i shout all of these things at her. at the stars. at the silent
sentinels of the forest.
until i am hoarse.
until tears blind my vision.
ah, but that is not your path. she says.
i know. i know. i know.
so, sweet child. she says.
as she again tips my chin to the vast dark of the night sky. as
she again runs fingers like mahogany across the base of my
throat. as her hands again, old and as weatherworn as the
mountains, guide my spine long; tailbone to the earth,
crown to the stars.
stop fighting it so.

you never could handle the way that my sadness moved
through your empty spaces; persistent until she echolocated
your own.
the way that my sadness delighted to find the relic of yours;
bereft and abandoned in her rusting suit of armour.
the way that my sadness danced affably up to where yours
sat within your wasteland of things forgotten and things
denied.
the way that mine delighted to find something that bound
us.
so you writhed and wiggled away.
you built higher walls and a more elaborate labyrinth of
defences.
and then, just in case my sadness could climb those walls
and navigate those mazes, because she is wily after all, a
trickster and a clever one at that, you tucked your sadness
away in the deepest cave in the furthest reaches of your
emotional mountain ranges.
i thought you couldn't handle my sadness, but it turns out
that you refuse to handle your own.

thirty

what do you hate? she asks.
and this one makes me writhe in discomfort; all of my early
conditioning with oppressive but well meaning aunts and
church groups rising to the surface, tentacles of belief
systems that were never supposed to be mine twining
around me to pull me back into a place that never should
have been mine.
hate is a strong word. hate isn't for good christians. hate isn't
what well mannered ladies do. i reply.
those aren't your words, she admonishes, that is what they
told you.
and she's right. of course, she's right.
so, in a rush, i scream:
i hate the way i was raised.
i hate that no one looked at the child i was and connected me
to the the teachings i needed.
i hate that my earliest memories are of being a burden.
i hate that my nose bleeds and bleeds and bleeds because i
have forgotten how to cry.
i hate that i have felt, my entire life, like i need to take care
of everyone else.
i hate that i have been ripped from roots that i only know in
cellular memory.
i hate that i barely know who i am.
i hate that i fully know who i am, but don't know how to
bring that truth to this earth.
i hate this reconciliation process of finding the teaching in
each wound. because, while the teachings are so good,
giving me shape, the wounds still hurt so much.

i hate that everyone tells me to choose love and yet they cannot see that with every tooth and nail, every breath and heartbeat, every fight that i choose, and with every day that i stay, i am choosing love.

i hate that everyone tells me to choose light when what i really want is the dark.

the dark.

the holy mother.

the crunch of bone between my teeth as i gnaw my way to marrow.

running the rough skin of my clawed hands over wild animals and even wilder earth.

pressing my belly, my throat, and the length of my body against soft moss or dank muck to feel the resonance of those spaces, hers and mine, teeming with invisible life.

what i really want is the dark.

the holy mother.

so yes, oh yes, i will allow my hate.

my anger.

my grief and my rage.

i will grieve and rage for who i was,

for who i never got to be

and for who i am learning to be.

i will welcome the dark.

the holy mother.

me.

meet her in the forest.
lay at her feet.
she'll let you rest. for a while.
but then she'll go to work.
changing you.
challenging you.
pulling off each mask you have meticulously created.
unconsciously created.
inherited.
peeling off the skins that have amassed; some tough and
thick, some mottled and half-grown, none of them truly
your own.
she'll scrub you down like you're nothing more than a small
child.
and you are, in this form, no more than a small child.
and don't you forget it.
in this form, this human skin, you are a mere blink in the
sheer magnitude of her lifetime.
don't let that frighten you though.
let it humble you.
let it awe you.
let it muster exquisite tenderness and attention.
no more than a small child.
but also the absolute and pure potential of a small child;
every possibility and every potential is held, vibrant and
alive, in your framework of skin and bone, stardust and
soul.
you are sweet and small and insignificant in the scope and
extent of her time scale.
you are like a single seed carried on the breeze that flows,
sometimes soft and warm, sometimes ferocious and hard,
over the landscape of her body.

a single small seed.

tiny.

minuscule.

yet an entire ecosystem of possibility is held tight,
contained, waiting within.

such seemingly insignificant packaging for such dormant
magic.

a single small seed.

looking for purchase.

a place to extend roots down into something fecund while
unfurling up towards something infinite.

single and small.

reconciling the polarity.

honouring the process.

softening into existence.

meditations on grief:
it comes in waves.
it cannot be chased off with the weaving together of vibrant
yellow and burnished copper beads.
it can be wedged, rolled, pinched and pressed into clay.
it can be sated with raindrops sipped from the sharp thorns
of a hawthorn.
it will crawl into bed with you, companionably, as you lay
your heavy bones down to sleep. only to wake you to your
own sense of panic, futility and utter sadness in the darkest
hours of the morning.
it loves the rain and the smell of damp, decaying leaves.
it takes your breath away with the sheer desperation and
tenderness you suddenly feel to live in a world as
remarkable as it is horrible.
it heightens everything.

thirty-three

how soft can you be with what still hurts?
how soft can you stay in the face of what will hurt?
how much softness can you allow when everything in you is
screaming to brace for impact?
tell me, what are your rituals for despair?

choose love they all say.
choose love.
but i am choosing love.
love that is just and holy.
love that is fierce and furious.
love that does not stand by, head in the sand, while
humanity hurts, the earth crumbles and bullies run
rampant.
love that is potent and straight from the mother.
i am choosing love.
wild love.
instinctual love.
loud love.
fearless love.
uninhibited, unabashed and unceasing love.
love that will not yield to new age paradigms or bend under
the weight of societal expectation.
love that does not fit into a neat and pretty package but
flows like a river; sometimes turbulent and imposing,
sometimes tranquil and inviting.
raw and unfiltered love.
revolutionary love.
i am choosing love.

thirty-five

wake up.
give my small fox with his deeply wounded paw his
medication. hug him tight and whisper into his hair, his
crown, reminders of how intelligent his body's healing
process is. run my hands over his shoulders and heart to
sweep away the sticky cobwebs that trauma leaves behind.
hug the resistant, yet wanting to soften, body of my wolf
child. watch in sleepy eyed awe as he launches himself from
zero to one hundred into the day ahead.
make espresso.
go outside and breathe in the rich cool of the morning air;
savouring these moments before the sun peeks over the
mountain and the temperature rises, turning the world
around me into an oven.
sip espresso as i shuffle from flower bed to flower bed and
around the yard noting what's new; blooms, spider webs,
weeds, tomatoes and peas, plums and pears. peeking into
the tangled messes of leaves in the hope of finding
something unexpected. plucking blooms here and there to
add to the drying rack.
and then my children tumble out the door; a riotous act of
noise and will, determination and demands, chaos and
hunger.
and just like that, the spell of espresso and flowers, early
morning cool and contemplation is lifted.
until tomorrow.

thirty-six

you, with your old hazel eyes, tell me you think that you are
a glitch.
and you, with your eyes as blue and expansive as the prairie
sky, tell me that sometimes you don't want to live anymore.
and me, with my amber eyes, i'm lost.
i don't know what to do or how to help you.
so i fold my body around yours while you sleep, my forehead
pressed to your ear, my chin tucked against your heart, and i
whisper to you, to your sleeping sweetness.
i whisper prayers and promises.
i whisper offerings.
i barter.
i tell you that i lived and i need you to do the same.
i tell you how our hearts have shared a home in my body
and that to lose your heart would destroy my own.
i call in the ancestors, the guides and the angels and demand
that they hold you safe.
i tell you about how beautiful and kind and strong you are.
i tell you that you hold medicine that will one day be a
lifeline for someone else.
i tell you about how your laughter is like the sound of fresh
water bouncing off of pebbles and that it is the most
wonderful, nourishing sound in all the world.
i tell you that i love you.
that it's ok.
that being human is exquisitely hard and excruciatingly
beautiful.
i weave words and whispers and love over the sweet
heaviness of your sleeping being.
i press my hand to your beating heart until its cadence is
imprinted on my palm.

and i love you.
and love you.
and love you.

where do you hate yourself? she asks.

here. i say.

and i grab handfuls of the soft tissue of my breasts. breasts
that have been with me, no, have betrayed me in the ways
they have made me visible since i was just thirteen.

and here. i add.

as i squish the gentle curve of my belly. because the world
has told me that fat is meant to be loathed and still, even
after all of this waking up, i believe it.

and here.

as i gesture to my throat where so long my truth was stuck,
caught, blocked and trapped that even now, *even now*, when
words and truth and power tumble so freely, i hold a
residual hate for the weakness that once held me captive.

and here. and here. and here.

i don't even need to think.

no pause or consideration.

here, here and here.

i can poke and prod and point to every fault, flaw and
weakness.

like my body is some prize animal not quite ready for the
local fair.

but now? she asks.

as she tips my chin towards the dark of the night sky.

as she runs fingers like mahogany across the base of my
throat.

as her hands, old and as weatherworn as the mountains,
guide my spine long; tailbone to the earth, crown to the
stars.

now you stop.

you stop playing these games.

you stop playing that you are merely human.

now you rise in remembrance of who you really are.
of *what* you really are.
now you honour this vessel for what it is; your container
through which both who and what you are must flow.
now you wake fully into creation.
and so it is.

thirty-eight

you were just a story i told myself.
now you are a story i can stop telling myself.

thirty-nine

i hope that my words land, soft and fresh like spring rain, in your heart.
i hope that you feel the vibration, the resonance, of my work, but respect that it has taken me a lifetime to get to this place before deciding to assume it as your own.
i hope that you do your work.
i hope that you shake off the weight of victimhood, misery and fear.
i hope that you make a pilgrimage to the core of who you are.
i hope that you move and love and live and breathe from your own vital truth, heart, spirit and soul.
i hope.
but it's not up to me.
it is up to me to hold space, hope, as vast and as holy as the dark starry night sky.
it is up to me to do my work.
to show up, over and over and over again, at the altar of my own heart; listening to, honouring, my soul's whispers.
it is up to me to lay myself bare at the feet of my highest self, offering this physical existence as a conduit for something so much bigger than i will ever fathom with this thinking mind.
it is up to me to approach this lifetime, and all within it, with a reverence rooted to the core of the earth and lit from the furthest reaches of the universe.
it is up to me.
and so hope flows into hard work. hard work flows into honouring. and honouring finds her way back to hope.
the circle continues; not unbroken, no. but stitched here and patched there, the circle continues.
hope. hard work. honouring.

animal characters create a form of simple contained
wisdom and these universal truths illuminate the human
condition throughout the ages.
then, granted a clarity of vision, we begin to see the world in
all of its magical wonder.
inside the body we unearth fresh and unrestricted vision.
imagination.
and we are seduced towards the ground.
but nobody believes.
because that is how grown-ups are.
nobody believes.
because we are unwilling, blind, to discover how common,
how repetitive, the rhythm of weakness in humankind.
nobody believes.
because we meet, desperate to be admired, but, alone or
together, cannot hear anything.
the lack of humanity in a world where items are the only
things of importance.
where we are constantly engaged in counting but we fail to
appreciate the beauty.
so i sit with just a wish.
just a wish.
the remarkable essence contained in the heart; invisible to
the eye yet articulated, turned loose, by those who return to
their wild.
myself included.

forty-one

my teeth feel sharp.
they ache.
growing pains, perhaps.
but i cannot tell if it is poison or nectar that wants to spill
from my lips.
i want vengeance.
i yearn for someone to pay.
but who?
and how?
by spitting my poison?
by weaving my nectar?
no.
or maybe.
but everything is too murky.
too sharp.
too full of aches and pains.
so i wait.
i watch.
i listen.
i trust wholly, holy, my own wisdom, magic and power.
because, what else is there?

forty-two

how did you get here?
where did it begin?
she asks.
i listened to their stories.
i say.
i listened so closely that their stories became my own.
that their stories became the stories i told myself.
it all became a story i told myself.
and now?
she asks.
now i tell my own story.
i say.

forty-three

hazey days.
like my head and my heart.
these liminal spaces,
transitional spaces,
are as gratefully received as they are bewildering.
be gentle.
move softly.
listen closely.

forty-four

i collect rocks.
no, i gather rocks.
still not right.
would you judge me as too strange if i said that the rocks are
collecting me?
anyway, it doesn't matter.
we, the rocks and i, we find each other.
down at the river. in the shallows of my favourite spring fed
lake. peeking out from the borderlines of lush mossy beds.
at the top of a waterfall that thunders away in an
inexplicable prairie expanse surrounded by mountains.
we find each other.
and always i stoop to scoop them up with a soft "oh hello
you."
i feel their weight and the contours of their evolution
against my palms.
i press them to my cheek or to my lips in order to feel their
coolness.
i see where they hold light and where they hold shadow.
and i listen.
i listen.
to see if they are mine or if i am theirs.
and lately i find myself gathering words the same way.
or again, maybe it is the words that are gathering me.
still, just like the rocks, the words and i find each other.
and just like the rocks, i explore them. testing weight and
contours, temperature, light and shadows.
and then i listen.
i listen to the way they feel.
and i watch the ways that they gather.
the way murmuration slips into susurration.
and how fertility dances, deep and low, into fecundity.

lush, of course.

verdant too.

potent and holy.

whisper and murmur.

unabashed.

soft.

rising.

thrumming.

awakening and remembrance.

ancient.

the words gather; as though my marrow is filled with them
and they drip steady into my veins.

or maybe as if the collage of my world is made up of them
and every so often i see through the veil of my waking world
to catch one or two.

but here, now, the words are gathering; rustling about on
the periphery of my conscious my mind, they make just
enough noise for me to know that they are there but not
enough yet for me to catch them.

forty-five

i can feel her; this new me.

no, that's not right.

she isn't new.

she's a remembrance.

she's an awakening.

she's something old as earth and i am but a blink in the timescale of her evolution.

and like a howling wind, she's on the move.

like a bird caught in a house, throwing itself against the perceived escape of a window pane, her frantic wings beat their cadence against my insides.

i feel her try on my heart, then slam herself against the confines of my ribcage; a tantrum against this space that is not yet expansive enough for her.

she stretches ferociously through the length of my spine; her lioness roar demanding more light, more energy; keening the snail's pace of my human capability to release and to create space.

she stomps her way through my being; a wildfire of spirit, clearing the undergrowth, the brambles, and the deadfall.

burning all the way back to fertile ground, seeking sacred space to plant the seeds of who she wants me to be, she leaves the the thick smoke of my emotions and belief systems hanging heavy in her wake.

i can feel her; my homecoming.

but her waking is an agony.

like a birth: wave after wave of unknowing, wave after wave of release, wave after wave of surrender.

like a death: wave after wave of unknowing, wave after wave of release, wave after wave of surrender.

forty-six

do you feel the melancholy?
the hiraeth?
the odd flutter of hope for something you cannot quite put
the words to?
the moon, love.
the moon is filling my head and now is lingering, heavy and
swollen, in my heart.
be tender, i remind myself.
be brave also.
listen closely to the whispers and notes, the nudges and
entire symphonies, singing through the spine of your
celestial body.
but mostly be bravely tender,
tenderly brave,
with your swollen moon heart.

that summer the lightning ran down the mountain.
the ditches ran rampant with wild roses in bloom; the pale
pink and brilliant fuchsia of the flowers amplified against
inky swaths of asphalt.
that summer.
the summer you walked the tightrope of desire and duty.
the summer i burned like holy fire; awake, alive, yearning,
seeking, keening, screaming.
screaming for more fuel.
shrieking my banshee song.
desperate and clinging, clawing, to anything that might
offer me purchase.
that was the summer i found myself at the diamond willow,
peering up at a crow's nest tumbled unceremoniously into a
tangled junction of branches.
and like a flood, a sharp intake of breath, i remembered the
dream from thirty years prior.
my six year old self standing in front of a diamond willow.
that same tumultuous gathering of sticks masquerading as a
nest.
and one giant black crow perched on the edge.
i remembered.
remember.
re-member.
her great inky black beak dipping into her nest and
emerging with two marbles: one milky white and one
startling blue.
i reached out for them, my hand pale and small in
comparison to this crow queen, and as she gave them to me
i, fast as a lightning bolt, sure as one too, popped them in
my mouth and swallowed them whole.

providing a safe space in my own belly.

warmth and nourishment too.

and that summer, thirty years later, was when i realized, i am the thing with wings.

inky black and iridescent they rustle against my frame.

i am the one who sees.

that summer we slammed, cataclysmic, tectonic, into one another.

you chose duty.

i chose both the agony and the ecstasy of awakening.

you erased me.
put up your walls, stopped taking my calls, and softly,
quietly, denied my existence.
and there is nothing i can do, because it was just you and me
on this island.
but you left.
you left.
and now it is just me; party of one on an island built by two.
and i don't know what to do.
i have wept and howled and raged.
i have set fire to the things that can hold flame.
i have asked the things with wings to carry me high so that i
might have a better view of it all.
i have asked the things with roots to grant me safe passage
down into the deep dank dark so that i might receive the
nutrients created by our decay.
i have sat, numb and confused, weaving the few threads you
left with the ones i find in dreamspace, trying to make a
complete picture out of something that never was complete.
because you left.
you left.
you didn't hesitate.
you didn't look back over your shoulder.
you didn't pause in your step.
i know this, because i watched.
i watched you go.
i watched you slip away like a snake in the grass; quiet and
fast, fluid and sure.
i watched you until you were nothing but a speck on the
horizon; so distant that i could no longer tell if it really was
you or my eyes playing tricks on my hopeful heart.

i watched.
because, like a child, i didn't think you would actually go.
i couldn't believe you would go.
i wouldn't let you go.
but just like a snake in the grass, you disappeared.
and now there is nothing left of us but a handful of
memories floating like specks of dust in a sunbeam; there
when the light slants across them just right but gone again
before i can be sure.
i needed an ending.
i need an ending.
something, some way, to pull this altogether and make
meaning from what was.
but you disappeared.
and you erased me.
and these here again, gone again motes of memory are all
that remain.
what i remember.
no ending.
what i remember is all that remains of the island we built
together.

untangle your knots.
my new drum, the one with the spots, the one that is
definitely masculine, whispered insistently to me as i wove
him into creation; untangle your knots, untangle your
knots, untangle your knots.
incessantly.
over and over again: untangle your knots.
in that almost taunting way that the masculine can have;
where they try to be tender and supportive but then the
bravado takes over and it becomes this coaching kind of a
chant that feels aggravating and against the grain.
untangle your knots.
still, who am i to not listen to such a clear message? from the
medicine keeper of a drum no less.
so i swallowed my objections.
i shelved my resistance and my hesitance to take masculine
directives.
and i opened myself to the untangling.
and that very night my student, who is actually a wolf
pretending that he is a man, told me "honesty is love."
and so that's where i start.
my first knot.
honesty is love.
honesty is not failing others. or disappointing them. or
letting them down.
or maybe it is, but then that is their knot to untangle and not
mine.
because honesty is love.
self love.
so i untangle; exploring the many twists and turns and then
teasing apart the tangles of honesty as love.
because this knot has been an entire lifetime in the making.

an entire lifetime of ignoring self for others.
an entire lifetime of not quite telling lies in order to put others first, but also an entire lifetime of not being completely honest either.
and as i work, head bent low, fingers deep in the guts of this knot, i see more knots showing up.
it's as though they have heard what i am up to and the medicine that i have agreed to swallow and now they too want to be untangled; they too want to be relieved of the deep and heavy ache held within their bellies.
so here's me, untangling and cursing and laughing.
shaking my head and twitching my hide and untangling some more.
an entire lifetime up to this point of making knots and an entire lifetime ahead of untangling them.

fifty

here we are.
waking from a long slumber.
a forced slumber.
a winter cycle that could not, would not, be denied.
here we are.
shaking dust from our shoulders.
blinking cobwebs from our eyes.
breathing breath, sweet and deep, into the thawing
mountains of our lungs.
here we are.
eager and ready to see which seeds will sprout and which,
buried too deep or maybe, perhaps, just not meant to be,
will add their decay to the richness of our soul's soil.
here we are.
as it was in the beginning and so it will be in the end.
here we are.
sinew and bones and flesh.
hearts beating loud and strong;
a cacophony of song that cannot be ignored;
a primal rhythm that knows the way.
holy giants in sacred, waking, feminine form.
here we are.

unearth your stories.

for your own well-being, yes.

but also for the aching hearts and spirits that need the
medicine, wisdom and fellowship pieces that only your
stories hold.

unearth your stories.

hold them,

dripping and dank or light and lovely,

for the world to see.

for the world to receive.

unearth your stories.

offer your medicine.

fifty-two

attune to what feels right.
what feels right.
what feels like nourishment.
what feels like tallow and marrow melting over your tongue
and the crunch of bones between your teeth.
there's receiving the holy communion of the grandmother,
the crone, as her forest dwelling body softens in my belly
and her mycelium dances through my being.
or insisting to my resistant wolf that he let me rub his back
as he tearfully confesses his fears and perceived failures, as
he cries and howls out a song that is much too old and much
too heavy for such a small beast. so i run my hands the
length of his spine and the distance between his shoulder
blades; desperately trying to scour the heavy shadows, the
tar-like doubt, from a back too small to carry such weight.
or there is the soft heaviness of my sleeping fox against my
back as he snorts and sighs his way through his dreamscape.
and there is admitting that some of this, most of this,
human experience is so fucking messy and sticky and
confusing. and then not immediately feeling ashamed for
not blindly, bypassingly, whitewashing it all with gratitude.
and not having answers.
not having answers but anchoring to an internal compass
set to what feels right in this moment and then the next one
and then the one after that.
moment by moment, what feels right.

fifty-three

you place the remains of your ancestors in birds nests. this
makes sense. a safe space. a soft space. a hatching space.
and you keep arranging your collections of bones and
stones.
seeking patterns and sense, codes and messages.
reading between the lines.
seething between the lines.
seeking between the lines.
you kiss raindrops from the barbed hawthorn branches
thinking that that might quench your heart.
and it does. for a while.
but then you find yourself laying in bed and, as you pretend
your way to sleep, feel your tongue pressed against your
teeth and wonder if you're doing it right. if you're wearing
this human form properly.
and then you wake up to everything happening in three's.
three stags cross the yard.
three times the murmuration of cedar waxwings thunders
overhead.
three times you walk into that same wall.
and it's all so bizarre.
you look at your children and recognize them so completely
and also wonder who the fuck they are and where they came
from.
why did they choose you?
but now you've circled back to how bizarre it all is.
so you curse your seeking nature just as much as you bless
your seeking nature.
then you swirl your whiskey and whisper a toast and a
prayer to the mountain tops before you are snapped back to
the present moment by the demand from a small blue-eyed
fox for his bedtime lavender milk.

the story goes that sedna was thrown overboard by her own father.
that as she clings to his vessel, he chops off her fingers.
one by one.
one by one, until she can no longer cling to the hope of his change of heart and she sinks into the salty and frigid deeps of the sea.
the story goes that her severed fingers became the first sea creatures.
the story goes that she was spiteful and would withhold the bounty of the sea.
but lately i find myself wondering: was she spiteful or was she wise?
did she withhold the bounty of the sea as punishment? or did she, wise lady of the briny depths, simply know when her water bound kin had extra to share with those up there on the land and when there was simply nothing else to give?
or perhaps she could not bear it, every now and again, to watch the family that took her in be severed from each other in the same way that she had been from the family that sentenced her? was she tired and exasperated at those that would cut her to her core, casting her alone and bereft to the sea, only to then be expected to provide them with their meal ticket? was she fucking fed up with a patriarchy that threw her asunder but also told tales, sob stories really, of how spiteful she was?
i don't know.
but her voice is coming to me again.
a rumble of water moving over rock.
a rumble of water churning stones and boulders over and against each other.

and she, in that deep sea swirling, seething voice of hers, is reminding me of things.

stirring remembrance far older than the sinew, bone and flesh i wear in this lifetime.

older than any lifetime i can summon in fact.

so i throw handfuls of irish moss into my bath.

dulse and bull kelp too.

sinking my body into the salty, fetid brine, i dance my fingers down through the currents. imagining them, myself, as shape-shifting selkies; here again, gone again, in human form.

sinking myself into my own watery depths.

wondering how the story would go if sedna had been allowed a voice.

slivers of light, caught above the rugged waveform of
mountain silhouettes and beneath seemingly endless banks
of clouds.
and a wolf pup of a boy who will spend eleven hours on his
skis, cheeks rosy from all that wild fresh air, eyes twinkling,
and still, *still*, not want to come in; fierceness and
determination the warp and weft of his bones.
and spinning the web of my story.
and the delight in a day of working with my hands. work
that is good and true and creating the ripples to call in new
outlets for creation, for sharing my heart with the world.
and the first tiny loose tooth for my blue-eyed fox; the way i
cried and laughed at this new milestone for my littlest
creature.
and making a list of the names for our future farm animals.
because, yes, we will leave the city. and, yes, we will have a
ridiculous herd of beasts to love.
and letting go. and letting go. and letting go.
and floating, free and easy, full of faith, in grace. but not too
easy. or at least not all the time.
no bypassing.
because my deepest teachings, blessings, and growth come
at the hands of the hard times and a holy capacity to
witness; from the faith that must be cultivated to endure
such times.
and the fortitude to thrive in this sweetly excruciating thing
called being human.
and offering myself, completely, to this life and to this work;
knowing that i won't do it perfectly or quickly, but that i will
keep going, collecting my breadcrumbs and honouring my
path.
dear universe: more of this. all of this.

fifty-six

it's ok to have boundaries.
limits.
thresholds.
it's ok to be disappointed.
to be fed up.
to recognize that someone offered you their best and to
know that, for you, it wasn't enough.
to recognize that someone never will offer you their best
and to know that that too isn't enough.
to burn your bridges.
and maybe the fire will warm you, maybe it will light your
way, or maybe it will consume you a little bit or entirely.
but you can burn that fucking bridge anyway.
to close doors.
because maybe when one door closes another one opens.
but definitely when one door closes you have made it clear
what is no longer welcome in your temple.
to know for sure.
to not know for sure. so you act now and beg forgiveness
later.
to not know for sure. so you take your sweet time
deciphering where the nudges are guiding you.
it's ok.
it's all ok.

fifty-seven

an expanse of snow and forest.
the sharp spine of mountains slicing through the clouds.
a sudden tenderness in my heart towards all of my
unanswered and answerless questions.
and then one of my small suns tumbles down a snowy cliff
and i must free him from the thicket of willows that have
claimed him as their own.
life is happening.
the miracles in the mundane.
the mundane in the miracles.
it's all happening.

fifty-eight

take a moment.
lay your body down, belly to belly and heart to heart, with
the earth; not like lovers, but the way a child falls asleep,
heavy and safe, fully surrendered, against their mother's
body.
now rest your cheek on a patch of moss.
or a bed of leaves.
or a thicket of clover.
or a mess of golden larch needles.
rest your head.
let your vision rest, loose and unfocused, as well.
and then wait, quietly.
breathe, quietly.
soften, quietly.
do this often enough and i promise you that you too will see
the thin places, the thresholds, between worlds.
do this often enough and i promise you that you too will
become the threshold between worlds.

fifty-nine

why don't they show up for me? i ask.
they know you're strong, so they think that you don't need
help. she replies.
well i fucking do. i retort.
then tell them that. she replies.
i don't want to be a bother. i mumble.
exactly. she snorts, as mirth dances across her ancient eyes.

sixty

if the earth herself is in a constant state of both creation
and destruction, why would you expect any less of your own
human self?
trust then,
little one,
the ebbs and flows,
the tearing down and the rebuilding,
the truth and the effort in your cyclical nature.

sixty-one

we are born knowing magic.

knowing that we are brave.

knowing that our body is simply an extension of our soul.

we are born knowing magic.

resonant and receptive.

listening and honouring.

knowing magic.

magic is our birthright and returning to magic is our work.

sixty-two

i didn't know my limitations.
i couldn't breathe.
i can't breathe.
and then the rainbow of a trout lands soft against my ankle.
and just like that,
with a howl of laughter and relief,
i land back in my body.
i land, back in my body.
grateful for the shimmering sliver of a teacher in trout
form.
grateful for the quiet moments when my mind isn't reeling
and my heart and spirit aren't searching.
grateful for the density of my body in this cold mountain
water.
and this is how i kiss this day good-bye; prayers of gratitude
spilling from my lips, my throat, my palms and my heart.

sixty-three

stillness does not mean stagnation.
retreat does not indicate defeat.
hearing does not necessarily equate listening.

sixty-four

as we walk in the river he stays up on the bank; keeping pace with us as we move upstream, only venturing down to the water to occasionally caress his hands along the surface.
as he traipses through the long grass, he collects a bouquet of wildflowers for me.
red clover.
buttercup.
a daisy that i am pretty sure is a type of noxious weed.
something purple that i can't identify; delicate bell-shaped blooms dangling from a fragile stem.
yarrow. always yarrow.
and we move.
my one boy in the water. boisterous and loud, diving right in. demanding to be seen. willing the world to match his energy and resolve. a little and incredible force of nature.
and one boy up on the bank. on the outskirts, an outlier, but still moving in parallel with us. slower paced, quieter, uncovering treasures the other one misses.
one hazel-eyed boy, one blue.
one yang and one yin.
two halves of my heart.

what would you say to her if she had lived? she asks.
i take a deep breath in.
as my heart slams into the cage of my ribs.
as my whole being reaches for she who did not live.
and i say:
i would tell her to never tuck her chin, bow her head or close
her eyes when she is photographed or in conversation. that
there is no need to play at demureness or patriarchal
notions of purity. keep your eyes open and level baby girl.
let them see your fire and purpose. show them that you are
no shrinking violet. let them know, through the amber
green gold of your eyes, that you aren't of this earth. let
them know, through the amber green gold of your eyes, that
you come from a rich tapestry of medicine women.
i would tell her to stand up straight. not because it lifts her
breasts or flattens her stomach or makes her more palatable
to society's eye. but stand up straight my child because your
spine is your strength; the channel of your matrilineal line.
because your spine carries a raging river of life and love,
knowing and healing, power and potency. because your
spine is how i will move through you when i am gone.
i would tell her to always listen to her heart. trust what you
know and feel over what you are told. never dull your
intelligence and keen wit to placate the masses.
i would tell her that nothing is permanent. sweet girl, if you
need to or if you want to, you can re-create yourself infinite
times over.
i would tell her to work hard because the world needs her
medicine.
i would tell her that she is my heart in conscious form.
that she is the delirious joy of the divine made manifest.

i would tell her a thousand things.
but mostly, with my words and with my life, i would tell her:
you are loved.
you are whole.
and you matter.

sixty-six

somewhere along the way to adulthood we lose the ability to
tell our stories; to honour them and then release them.
instead we bury our stories.
we hide them deep under layers of guilt and shame and fear.
we turn away from them, leaving them to fester.
we let them take hold and grow roots; dictating, directing,
the terms of our existence.
we are supposed to be storytellers.
not just for entertainment or education, but for healing
process; yours and mine.
you?
what are your stories?
what longs to be shared?
what needs to be heard?
what do you carry in solitude that should be shared in
community?
unearth your stories.
dripping and dank, twisted and malignant, or light and
lovely; dig up the bones, the detritus and the roots of what
has made you.
because when we heal the self, we heal the whole.

to those that care so deeply.

to those that are showing up, doing the work within and without, and letting the magnitude of both their feminine strength and softness shift the landscape of this world.

to those that are teaching the next generation to do the same.

to the sacred space holders.

to those with the shining eyes.

to those with the scarred-up hearts; the hearts that they continue to come home to, to listen to.

to those that protect with a ferocity that stops others dead in their tracks, yet still walk gently, hand in hand, with compassion, healing, and forgiveness.

to those that have burned themselves to the ground only to rise stronger, again and again, from their own ashes.

to those that have floundered and flailed through a wasteland of inhospitable terrain, but still held their chins high and hearts open.

to those that pull off the masks and layers and chains imposed by a society that wants to fit them into a neat and tidy box.

to those that tend to this vast and tender garden of humanity.

to those that weep, howl, rage, and roar. and then, shaking the heaviness from their bones, dance and laugh from their bellies and sing their soul songs and love and love and love.

to those that embrace both the mess and the glory of this existence.

thank you.

my gratitude heart is for you.

for us.

thank you.

let's live like the fuzzy bumble bees and the pink peony
flowers; improbable and delightful and purposeful and
doing our own thing.
because what other thing is there to do?
and let's wear quartz crowns and angel wings of foraged
feathers.
we'll wrap love notes around the sparkling stones, the round
stones and the smooth stones. we'll roll love notes and tuck
them into the stones with the holes in them. and then we'll
leave our love note stone people everywhere; breadcrumbs
for the lovers, the seekers and the dreamers to find.
let's sleep in and wake up slowly; letting dreams, half
remembered, tumble from our mouths and hearts.
and let's do a whole lot of nothing.
nothing at all.
we'll pretend we're hiding in full site and laugh and marvel
at the hubbub of all the people who are still asleep; blessing
their journey, cause we've been there, while joyfully holding
space for process, theirs and our own.
let's fall in love.
and fall in love.
and fall in love.
and tomorrow let's do it all again.
but let's not hold any expectations.
because tomorrow might be entirely different.
tomorrow might hold some new glittering morsel of magic.
and so, my dear, let's be certain we don't close ourselves off
from that potential.
let's breathe it all in and love it all out.
let's see it, glittering and magic or dank and magic, and
throw our heads back with ecstatic joy that we get to see at
all.

sixty-nine

she tells me, you are prolific.
and i respond, but i feel tiny and human and raw.
and she, this selkie lioness woman, she laughs.
this sister keeper i've never met.
this laugh i've never heard.
this laugh that i imagine as light and ethereal, like the peal
of a thousand crystal bells, but secretly hope for it to be loud
and brazen, straight from the belly, just like my own.
and my brain grapples, isn't the world a strange place?
but my heart pipes up, vehemently, the world is a magic
place.
a magic place.
where watery mermaid mamas find mossy forest mamas
and a sisterhood that was agreed upon, long before bodies
took shape, takes light.
where community is called into existence from the
vibration of heart song and we weave each other, in
whatever capacity we can, into the fabric of each other's
existence.
where we play midwife to each other's hearts and spirits
and, in return, are midwifed further into our own truth.
where we grow each other up.
where we rise together.
in high vibration, fierce determination and the tender
unyielding love of our mama hearts, we rise together.

get close, closer, to your wild woman ways.

to your wild woman knowing.

get close, closer, to the animal instinct of your body.

get close, closer.

these times call for you.

wide awake,

unmasked,

wild woman and animal instinct,

you.

get close, closer.

let my words, beautiful and potent and holy, rise up from
the creative centre of my belly before tumbling from my
mouth; the same way that spring water rises, clean and
clear, from some unknowable depth before spilling down
the mountainside.
let my spirit contain within it the continuous dance of both
expansion and centering.
let me flow golden and liquid to the heavens, like sweet
honey light, while my roots drop deep to the crystal core of
the earth.
let my life be the altar of my vast and sacred heart.
and let my heart be an offering, a space holder, a wide awake
wisdom keeper, so that your heart may do the same.
and so it is.

seventy-two

i am circling in.
finely tuning.
becoming ever present to the ecosystems of my internal and
external landscapes.
and you know what?
sometimes i still pretend, still play, like i am here alone;
bereft, abandoned, by my source.
but, honestly?
i know better.
i do.
this environment, this me, physically, emotionally,
mentally, energetically, and spiritually, does not exist in
homeostasis.
this environment exists in flux.
in ebbs and flows.
in holy strength and human sorrow.
in grand production and healing retreat.
in star codes and sinew.
in sacred, *sacred*, form.
me.
this environment, this human landscape, this extension of
earth; me.
soft, like smoke, or things seen but not seen from the
periphery, i reach.
no, not reach, no grasping here.
soft, i extend.
soft, i open.
i release so that i may receive and i receive so that i may
release.
i return, always, to my dance with the divine.
to my dance as the divine.
feet aching, steps unknown, song unfamiliar, i return.

an altar of teeth.

gnashing teeth.

words catching on teeth; caught in deep disappointment.

confusion.

hurt.

teeth bared; snarling wild women momentarily wounded,
blind-sided, backed into a corner.

an altar of mourning.

of sitting, fully, with what is.

of tasting bitter medicine that is undeniably real, present,
and in power.

of waking up, not gently, not sweetly, but fast and hard.

and grief.

such grief.

today we sit with grief.

howling, teeth bared, we rage with our grief.

we mourn what is; what could have been.

but we stay close to the holy fire that is burning, has always
burned, in our bellies.

we stay close, get closer, to our wild woman knowing.

and then,

howling,

teeth bared,

full of love,

sacred strength blazing,

we fight.

we are waking further to our selves as sentient, conscious creators; as the weavers of our own fate.

because this is no longer the time to be battered about by strange energies, claiming to be the victim, trapped in a fear state.

because this is the time to wake up to an unwavering and potent faith.

because the web we are currently spinning, in fear or in love, directly impacts both our present and our future.

take the time to get clear.

take the time to consciously study the patterns, habits and beliefs you have blindly accepted, blindly allowed to shape your reality.

take the time to spiral in on the unique truth held in your wide awake heart; the purpose, dream and work of your life.

find space, get quiet, drop in to the divine darkness within, and map it all out.

dust the cobwebs from the hallowed giant of your heart and begin to weave your words, your dreams and your sacred gifts.

honour the growth and lessons of your past as you create a present and future that pulse with the crystalline truth of your heart, spirit and soul.

we are gently, lovingly, tending to the web of what is, but we are also weaving what will come to be; do not waste this gift.

we are creation.

we are waking up.

and so it is.

seventy-five

i can feel words thrumming in me.

no, that's not quite right.

they're stories.

i can feel stories thrumming in me.

big stories.

strong stories.

medicine stories.

wellspring stories.

they're filtering through me like so many motes of dust in a sunbeam.

but that isn't right either.

because how can i deem them dust and myself the sunbeam?

to be honest, these stories are far more ancient, more potent, more wise, than this human shape i wear.

and, to be honest, these stories frighten me almost as much as they exhilarate me.

because i'm not enough, my small self pleads.

but my wild woman throws her head back and howls with laughter at this notion and then leads me deeper into the forest.

because, silly child, you are everything.

these stories are threads, thousands of threads, and their strength has been tested, broken, and then rebuilt through the millennia.

these are stories that have been passed with reverence through millions of hearts.

these are the same stories though that have been spit from too many mouths twisted with fear.

endless iterations, in endless lifetimes.

and these stories?

these are the stories that weave me into existence.

she asks me how my sleep is.
oh good, i say.
but for the last little while i have woken up every morning
around three, i add.
she tells me that that is when the energy is shifting from
liver to lungs.
she tells me that the liver processes frustration, the lungs
process sorrow.
she tells me, gently, as though speaking to a small child, that
waking up at this time can be an indicator that i am stuck in
these emotions.
i nod politely, small smile.
but i feel her words ripple through my heart.
it's three a.m. and i am in bed with frustration and sorrow.
it's three a.m. and i am praying for release.
it's three a.m. and i am dancing with grief to the songs of
loss i wrote myself; the resonance of the melody sits heavy,
like silt, in my body.
it's three a.m. and i am clinging to the goddess; whispering
my penance in her ear, while howling my truth to the full
moon of her heart.
it's three a.m. and i can feel every wild part of me alive and
on the prowl; keening and wailing, seeking a way out.
it's three a.m. and the intuition of my body is like wildfire.
it's three a.m. and i am tired.

mind tells me:

you are a tangled mess.

you stand on a crumbling platform.

you are this, you are that.

but also you are not this and definitely not that.

you are too much.

you are not enough.

you love too much and deserve the way your heart is aching.

you feel too much and deserve the way your heart is aching.

you know too much and deserve the way your heart is
aching.

you should have stayed in your lane.

you don't belong here.

but heart whispers:

you are creation.

hush.

rest.

receive.

seventy-eight

i would dance to the cadence of your steady heart; learn its
rhythm as fully as my own.

or maybe i would drop my own thrumming honeybee heart
into your hands and watch the way you hold it; all gentle
calm and no sudden movements.

i would listen to your words.

no not those, no small talk.

your real words.

the ones that make their way up from deep within, fresh and
nourishing, wild and pure; a wellspring of words straight
from your source.

i would hold your head to the base of my throat, or maybe in
my lap, while i traced my fingers the length of your spine;
coaxing out and brushing away the slivers of your fear.

i would witness your awakening.

your remembrance.

your healing.

i crave your healing.

but instead i stand transfixed. immobile.

and like some great tethered beast, i can feel the weight of
my spirit straining against the ties of your resistance.

i beat my wings to tatters, like a moth, seeking the light held
prisoner inside you.

held prisoner from me.

i want to scream and shout and claw:

do you know what this is?

do you know who we are?

i want to turn the wild rumpus of my being loose on you.

to let her shake you and devour you and leave you stripped
bare.

to wake you.

to let her burn you to the ground so that you too can rise
from the ashes of who you were, of who you thought you
were supposed to be.
and now my ribs ache from holding my breath.
from holding my frustration.
and my bones have turned to rust.
and my wings are broken by the weight of you.

seventy-nine

let your heart declare dominion over your entire being,
while whispering softly to spirit:
i am yours,
i am yours,
i am yours.
do what you will with me,
i am yours.

crumble. crash. fall apart. disintegrate. unravel. fall to
pieces. shatter. break. crack. splinter. burst. rupture.
fracture. falter. tear. come apart at the seams. come undone.
explode. implode. burn. collapse. rage.
go ahead, do it.
but don't stay there; don't drape yourself in the cloak of
darkness and wear it like some twisted superhero's cape of
safety, trusting the low vibration that you know over the
high vibration that you have yet to meet.
honour the shadow side of growth.
because you need to know the dark to know that you are
meant to live in the light.
honour the vulnerability of allowing weakness.
because you need to feel frightened and tiny and not even
remotely strong in order to see how badly you desire love
and expansion and strength.
you need to know that you can burn your self to the ground,
time and again, so that you can rebuild stronger and cleaner
and clearer each time; with each rebuild spiralling in on a
truth that pulses straight from your own heart.
but don't forget to rebuild.
approach your wounds, your flaws, and your brokenness
with a gentle tenderness.
because they are the way in.
they are the way in, not a source of shame.
and when you see it, this way in, this window to the heart,
spirit and soul, do not hesitate.
jump in. go. build. rally. emerge. embrace. seek. explore.
expand. rise. evolve. thrive. mature. advance. progress.
grow. develop.
come home.

tonight i dance to grandmother spider's heartbeat.
tonight i sing down the moon.
tonight i sit at the feet of ereshkigal.
persephone and sedna.
the cailleach and the morrigan.
lilith.
crone.
and these dark women, these wisdom keepers, these holiest
of space holders, they burn through me.
they move like the earth through my being.
primal.
unstoppable.
burning, cleansing, purifying.
anything that i carry, anything that i hold, and anything that
i cling to that is not in resonance with this current iteration
of me, or with the spiral dance of evolution that i am on, is
held to the flame.
the destruction in their wake leaves me awestruck.
grateful.
rendered tiny yet heightened.
they stomp, dance and delight their way through my being.
their wildfire clears the undergrowth, the brambles, and the
deadfall, until they reach the fertile ground they seek; the
sacred space to plant the seeds of who i am to be, of who
they need me to be.
their fingernails tear the fear, resistance, and doubt from
my flesh.
their long fingers weave truth into my heart.
their voices sing gold into my spine.
their skin patching the places in my own that i have worn
thin.

their own hearts beat nourishment and courage into my
throat.

tonight it's me and a grandmother drum.

me and my blood and the moon.

me and the smoke.

me and these women.

me.

that i may release.

that i may receive.

that i may become stronger, richer, more courageous and
more clear on the path.

that i may birth the fecundity of my darkness into the light.

that i may be of service.

and so it is.

eighty-two

i show myself
to the sun.
and,
softly,
i let the tigers come.

you came to me in dreamspace.

of course you did.

you could not, would not, come to me in flesh and bone,
heart and marrow.

not then.

not now.

dreamspace has always been your preferred channel.

your safest space.

so of course, of course, that was how you touched me one
last time.

the familiar profile of you silhouetted in golden rays of
sunlight as you handed me a scrap of paper splashed with
promises to be upheld in another lifetime.

you came to me in dreamspace.

silhouetted in gold.

and just like that our crocodile tails untangled and we both
moved on.

until next time my friend.

you will plant many seeds.

some will grow.

some will not.

some will become something entirely unexpected.

larger perhaps.

or messier.

or more prolific than expected.

or maybe less than what was hoped for.

or invasive.

and so on.

but you keep planting your seeds.

re-seeding what you loved.

what worked.

what was good and provided nourishment.

what wasn't good but still provided nourishment.

weeding out what you know no longer or never was going to work.

planting and tending we go,

on and on,

until we reach the end.

eighty-five

everything,
e v e r y t h i n g,
is an iteration of either love or fear.
love frees us.
fear either enslaves us or allows us to enslave others.
be aware.
pay attention.
choose wisely.

the fascia in my back is stuck and my neck hurts. i say.
there is a triangle of exquisite pain from the base of my
skull out to the tip of my shoulder down to the heart of my
shoulder blade and back up again. on both sides. i add.
oh yes, she chuckles.
a manta ray has attached itself to your back.
what?
but who am i to question her ancient wisdom.
in the physical realm, i feel quite accomplished; an excellent
student of spirit, soul and self-study.
but with her? with her my wisdom feels infinitesimally
small; a mere flick of a feathery wing across the sheer
landscape of her timescale.
but i like manta rays. i stammer. unable to come up with an
intelligent query.
that's all well and fine, she says as she clucks her tongue and
shuffles away from me.
but they belong to the sea and not to your spine.
so i carry my manta ray around for a few weeks.
i ask it to leave, but it doesn't.
i try to smudge it away and stretch it away, but still it stays.
and then the full blood moon arrives.
the lunar eclipse too.
and just like that i see my manta ray, no longer mine, take
flight into the great starry sea that laps against these
mountain tops.
i see her swim the currents of the sky until she settles her
great bulk into the craters of the moon.
now i feel deep roots, black as night, reach through my skin.
moving through my fascia, my muscles and my bones, they
extricate other things, non manta ray things, that remain
unidentifiable; too gnarled and too layered to decipher.

and just like that the pain is gone.
i can sense whispers, reminders, of how to continue this
work.
but they're more felt, known, than heard.
so i listen and respond.
trust the knowing and ignore the judging, the rationalizing.
whole body, embodied listening.
whole body, embodied response.
whole body, embodied resonance.
spirit and soul, heart and mind:
listening.
responding.
resonating.

eighty-seven

i am fluent in shadow speak.
you were never mine to save.
i want to forgive you.

eighty-eight

i'm hungry.
she moans.
yowls.
yawns.
i'm hungry.
the words sound round to my ears.
heavy.
petulant.
a growling rasp offered around a mouthful of penance
never swallowed.
i'm hungry.
she hisses.
growls.
howls.
she's getting louder.
closer.
close enough now that i can hear the rough pads of her feet,
like sandpaper, as she paces back and forth.
close enough now that i can hear the way her heart beats in
my throat.
close enough now that i can hear the hum of electric light
along the warp and weft of her sinew and bones.
close enough now that i can feel her hand as my own hand
hammering the walls and looking for a way out.
close enough now that i can no longer tell who wears who.
i'm hungry.
she says.
as she licks my lips and dons my bones.

eighty-nine

i've never felt at home here. on earth.
i've found myself in places, both physically and out of body,
that my soul remembers and felt a certain kinship or sense
of arrival.
but not home.
i remember, in a way that is so deep and guttural i don't even
have words for it, a home.
a place of origin.
but what does one do with that?
how does one search for or connect to a home that is only
remembered in the most primal of ways?
a home that doesn't feel on this plane?
please tell me. i'd be mighty grateful.
so, rather than get tangled in my own existential ouroboros,
i practice.
i practice being home here.
in these mountains and forests, rivers and lakes.
in the hearts, love and delight of my children.
in the make up of my own sinew and marrow, muscle and
bone.
in the soft whispers and fervent banshee wails, the jubilant
songs and keening howls, of my guides and ancestors.
i practice.
and sometimes all that i can muster is to pretend.
but even in the pretending there is an element of practice.
i practice.
grounding. feeling. listening. reclaiming. reconciling.
i practice being a home.

ninety

fireweed came to me in dreamspace.
she beckoned me deep into a dark forest.
a blackened forest.
a forest that remembered burning.
her siren song, sweet and holy, showed me the way.
i did not stumble or waver.
i moved with ease.
with grace.
with knowing.
until there she was.
tall and brilliant.
inescapably vibrant.
on fire, but not.
and as the flames that were there, but also not, flickered
purple and orange along her petals, i could see her roots
rising and falling, pulsing with the beat of some unseen
heart.
and then she was in my heart.
and my heart had become the forest.
and i could remember burning.
and that caused my heart to stumble.
but i felt her whisper steady me:
i am here to reclaim and restore.

ninety-one

i pretended that these little blooms were all that stood
between me and the sun.

between me and the mountain.

between me and you.

i alternated, swinging like a pendulum, between the belief
in the sweetness of being protected by a flower and the folly
of thinking anything stands between me and, well,
anything.

do i need protection?

do i need to believe there is separation?

then i threw my head back and howled with laughter; great
heaving sobs of mirth rising from my belly and tumbling
raucously past my lips.

when i blinked my eyes back open i could feel that i too was
the mountain.

so with a great yawning gulp i too swallowed the sun and in
doing so i also became the sun.

but i will not become you.

you don't have enough meat on your bones or thunder in
your heart to nourish me.

and yet.

and yet, we are not separate.

and as i spin around on the perplexity of the being-one-
withness and the not-becomingness of the situation
between you and i, i find that i am getting dizzy.

so i lift my blooms back up and once again believe in their
strength to stand between us.

open to your innate wisdom.

wisdom that is stored, potent and sweet like honey, in the most sacred chambers of your heart.

wisdom that has danced through the stories of your ancestral line.

wisdom that has followed you from lifetime to lifetime, honing in on a strength and resonance that is crystalline.

wisdom that is willing you to heed its holy whisper.

call in movement, through dance and celebration of form, where too long there has been stagnation.

sing the praise of your grief and howl the profanities of your rage.

clear the debris.

in joy and in despair, clear the debris.

return to your wisdom.

and so it is.

ninety-three

i see
you decided
to grow flowers
from our decay.

ninety-four

current practice:
grief as endurance.
or is it the endurance of grief?
either way,
there is no room for parchment paper skin or a flimsy heart.

my kids are shooting pellet guns at pop cans out on this back
country road.
i found probably the last wild rose of the season, snapped a
photo and now sit at the edge of this dusty ditch trying to
coax my seized neck muscles back into the land of the
limber.
i turn my head this way and that, tuck my chin to my chest,
then drop each ear toward its corresponding shoulder.
breathe steady through the constant dull ache.
breathe steadier through the occasional sharp blade of pain
that arcs across my traps and up into the base of my skull.
i think about my sense of wild roses over the course of my
life so far.
i think about my sense of wild childhood versus that of my
children's.
i think about the responsibility of raising boy-identifying
children.
i think about how much i hate guns.
i start to spiral into worry over the state of the world, the
fate of the world.
so i haul myself up from the ditch and wander a ways
further up the road.
looking for more flowers.
listening to the wind rustled leaves and the caw of a crow.
trying to hold my head delicately on the aching mess of my
neck.
feeling good and feeling bad.
but feeling none the less.

ninety-six

we had to turn the furnace on today.
after living in an oven all summer it seems strange to need
artificial heat.
the sound of the fan is making my skin crawl.

{redacted}
the memory of you is making my skin crawl.

it rained last night.
heavy and hard against the roof.
the cool of it is making my skin dance.

the brambles of memory are particularly thorny as my head
swims with this moon.
but then the star speckled, velvet dark of the night sky is
especially sweet.

it is not one or the other.
it is
always
often
mostly
usually
typically
both.

ninety-seven

you came to me in dreamspace.
your preferred medium.
before.
during.
still.
we stood across from each other in a wasteland.
you would not look at me.
so i bared my teeth.
i shrieked.
howled.
roared.
why?
i pleaded.
raged.
why have you not held up your side of the agreement?
you shrugged your shoulders sadly, your eyes finally finding
mine, and simply said "i have".
and just like that you gave me your final gift.
all of my brokenness shifted from something sharp and
dangerous, something i kept harming myself on, slamming
myself into, to a potent and nourishing fire.
just like that, you became my catalyst.
just like that, my frustration, confusion and rage danced,
shapeshifted, into mourning, grief and a holy, holy
embodiment and understanding.
just like that, my clarity became crystalline.
thank you.
because of you i know that i am the one.
that i never needed it to be us.
i am the one.
i am.

when you died, my throat filled with smoke.

thick, acrid smoke.

i coughed and coughed and coughed, but it would not clear.

when you died, my bones already heavy with the grief of
anticipation became even heavier with the grief of
realization.

my bones turned to clay.

and now i find that the hardest thing about this grief is that
the world has not stopped.

the children still need to be fed and loved and tended. they
still bicker and move at a tumultuous, raucous, speed and
volume.

the groceries still need to be bought and the dog walked.

people still make small talk.

and to everyone and to all of the things i want to peel open
my chest and say look.

look at this.

can you truly not see how deep and raw this wound in my
heart is?

can you not just leave me so that i can tend to this pain?

but the world has continued to spin.

so i went today and painted deep dark slip into all the bone
white pots i pinched while i waited for you to die.

while the clay and i held vigil

vigil vessels.

maybe i'll give one to my mom. to each of my sisters. to your
daughter too.

maybe i'll smash them to pieces on the rocks at the river;
returning the clay back to her mother, allowing all of that
stored grief to be washed away.

ninety-nine

i want to scream.
i do.
i want to pierce the dulcet silence of this forest with my
banshee wail.
with my keening.
with my howls of desperation and of grief and of rage.
but every time that i open my mouth, nothing but the
twinkling of stars comes tumbling out.
and all of the sudden everything feels so heavy.
my body.
this earth.
this engagement with living.
and i begin to wonder when the spaces between my ribs
started to fill with rust.
and i try to remember when the tissue of my breasts started
to ache like this.
and bone by bone i sink into the forest floor.
i stare up at a brilliant canopy of emerald cedar fronds and
golden poplar leaves as my tears feed the mosses and
mycelia that wreathe my skull.
i have no answers.
but i can't quite be sure that i still have questions.
and what am i supposed to do with that?
so i relinquish myself to the forest floor and simply rest.

one hundred

today.
i am the prayer.
i am the treasure discovered and gratefully received.

i hate motherhood today.
this whole week in fact.
it feels too constrictive.
too full of chaos.
the drone of near constant noise is chafing at my heart.
the nagging belief that i'm doing more harm than good, that
i've damaged them, has her hands wrapped tight around my
throat.
and i keep looking over my shoulder to see if anyone has
caught on to the fact that i don't know what i'm doing.
but i also keep coming back to their faces; i love the
exquisite landscape of their faces.
the way the hazel-eyed one has a perfect triangle of freckles
on his left cheek and the blue-eyed one has thick straw
coloured lashes that i swear belong on a lion.
the way their skin is like velvet, covered with soft downy
hair, as it stretches over cheekbones and across the expanse
of their jawlines and foreheads.
i know the geography of their faces by heart.
i also know that this feeling won't last. it never does.
so for now, for now, i tuck myself away in my room.
i hide myself just as much as i find my self down at the
river.
i demand that we go on walks together to the forest to see if
the rain has woken up the mushrooms.
i remind myself that there are days where i can set my
mothering standard to simply keeping them alive and that
these are those days.
i remind myself that it is hard because it is growth; that
these tiny mirror humans are shining light onto the wounds
that i still need to heal in myself.

i remind myself that, even when i hate motherhood,
i am still so utterly in love with them as humans.

i will weep again.
rage will howl through my being, causing my fascia to ache
and my skin to tighten.
my heart will become heavy and weary in the framework of
my ribcage.
songs of grief will rise, thick and potent, from my pelvis,
my spine, my heart and my throat.
i will plead and beg for a home that i don't even know exists;
battling a longing and homesickness that can't be placed.
i will keen and wail and flounder and reel.
but today?
right now?
i have the alchemy of flowers becoming apricots.
i have a blue-eyed boy's sweet determination and dedication
to learning the art of tying shoelaces.
i have a hazel-eyed boy who is often more storm than sun,
but right now his light is shining bright and resplendent.
i have this breath.
and then one more.
i don't know what caused this shift; what planets aligned or
what tectonic plate shifted or what star blinked her last light
toward this earth.
but suddenly, just like that, for the first time in too long,
there is ease and light.
i know my spiral dance will spin me around through it all
again, moving me through the muck and the mire, the dank
fecundity found in the heaviness.
but right now i am dancing high in my heart.
i am head tipped back shrieking my delight.
i am unabashed laughter rising and tumbling from the
depths of my belly.

i am rich and i am rising; potent and holy, my wings
unfurled and gleaming.
right now?
i am.

i've been slamming into old hurts lately.
anger.
resentment.
sadness.
heartache.
grief.
a desolate re-mourning of things previously mourned.
it has been peculiar.
and tiring.
and emotionally so much.
so many memories filtering through.
but then today i was reminded that this is what it's like to
have grown a new boundary.
to stand within the new expanse of my landscape and watch,
as all of the things that my old self allowed slam into what
my current self no longer has time for.

i want to say something like
"may you only ever wrap yourself around the things that are good and worthy and reciprocal."
but that would negate the sheer volume of learning that can come from wrapping yourself around all of the things that are not good or worthy or reciprocal.
so, sweet love, may you wrap yourself mostly around things that are good and worthy and reciprocal.
but may you learn, tenderly and quickly, from the things that aren't.
and i sincerely hope that you harbour no shame or guilt in committing yourself to the things that aren't.
and if you do, may you recognize that shame or guilt and release it quickly.
because we are all just doing the best that we can with what we know in any given moment.
because as we know better, we do better.
because this is the messiness of being human.
stay soft, sweet beast.
listen closely and move gently, too.
because we all have wounds.

i touch the fever heat of my lips to the cool skin of my drum
and i listen.
i listen to the way she whispers into my mouth.
and as i listen, i see.
vibration translates to vision and i see.
i see women gathered. holding each other in circle. right
hand to their own heart, left hand to the dark side of their
sister's heart. hands to hearts, they throw back their heads,
unhinge their jaws, and swallow the sun.
i see women marching. endless rows. as they march they
turn their heads to the left and to the right. to the left, two,
three, four; mouths open wide as they spit hordes of bees,
swallows and ravens. to the right, two, three, four; mouths
open wide and they shriek the song of the earth as she both
consumes and gives birth to herself.
i see women birthing themselves into being. midwifing new
growth from the decay of who they once were; their death
rattles dance slow and deep, pelvis to pelvis, with their birth
songs.
i see women creating themselves out of scavenged
treasures; blooms and the desiccated husks of seed pods,
sun bleached bones and moth wings, feathers of every size
and hue, mosses and mushrooms, leaves and sticks and
stones.
i see women hefting great swords, mounting horses made
of mountain peaks, and nocking arrows onto bowstrings as
they all roar like the the milky way into battle.
i see women who are weary.
i see these same weary women straighten their spines,
signal their radiant defiance through the lift of their chins
and the fire in their eyes, while smoothing their human skin
over luminescent selkie bones.

i see women mending their broken places with mica and
tourmaline, garnet and pyrite, smooth river stones and
rough hewn granite. filling their worn too thin spaces with
glittering quartz and spar.
i see women being adorned, initiated.
i see women being adorned, celebrated.
i see women.
i see prayer in feminine form.
i see.
and so it is.

about kael:

i am a medicine woman. a shadow worker. a story teller.
i am here to teach, to heal and to guide, not by telling or
prescribing, but by openly, honestly, being.
thank you for sitting with me in this capacity; for leaning in
to our shared experiences, spaces and healing.
if there was one last thing that i could give you, it would be
this:

you are safe.
you are worthy.
you are whole.
you are enough.
and so it is.
and so it is.
and so it fucking is.

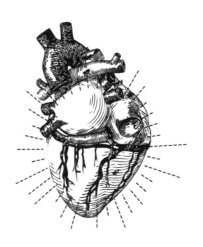

Lightning Source UK Ltd.
Milton Keynes UK
UKHW020049180220
358859UK00008B/283

9 780368 556432